Entry Level

Functional Skills

Information Communication Technology

(ICT) Entry Level 1, 2 and 3

Step-By-Step Guide

Office 2010 & Windows 7

By
Lorna Bointon

Qualiteach Education

D1322751

© Lorna Bointon, Qualiteach Education 2012

ISBN: 978-0-9565731-3-1

A catalogue record for this book is available from the British Library

Published by
Qualiteach Education
For more copies of this book, please email: contact@qualiteach.co.uk
Tel: 0800 612 5438
Web: www.qualiteach.co.uk

Printed in Great Britain

First Published   2012

Microsoft ® Windows®, Microsoft® Office, Microsoft® Office Word 2010, Microsoft® Office Access 2010, Microsoft® Office Excel 2010, Microsoft® Office PowerPoint 2010, Microsoft® Office Outlook 2010 and Microsoft® Internet Explorer are either registered trademarks or trademarks of the Microsoft corporation. Windows® is a registered trademark of Microsoft Corporation in the United States and other countries

Entry Level Functional Skills ICT is an independent publication and is not affiliated with, nor has it been authorized, sponsored, or otherwise approved by the Microsoft Corporation.

The companies, organisations, products, the related people, their positions, names, addresses and details used for instructional purposes in the manual and its related support materials on the Web are fictitious. No association with any real company, organisations, products or people are intended nor should be inferred. Although every precaution has been taken in the preparation of this book, the publisher and author assume no responsibility for errors or omissions. Neither is any liability assumed for damages resulting from the use of this information contained herein.

Qualiteach Education

Credits

Author
Lorna Bointon

Editor
Richard Bointon

IMPORTANT

ABOUT THIS BOOK

Other Functional Skills resources at Level 1 and Level 2 are available from Qualiteach Education. Schools and colleges may purchase a site licence allowing unlimited photocopying of training materials, such as build-up exercises, practice papers and reference guides.

Contents

Section 1 ▶

Use
ICT

Using ICT

Start & Shut Down an ICT System

What does it mean?

An ICT system can be a computer or a mobile phone. The information stored on a computer or a mobile device needs to be kept safe by making sure that no-one else can access it without your permission (this is called unauthorised entry or hacking). Information stored in an ICT system can be made more secure by logging in with a username and password.

It is important to shut down an ICT system correctly by first logging off any websites that are open and closing all documents and open windows. Closing an ICT system correctly helps to prevent hardware problems.

Help Sheet - Handy Tips

Start a computer

- Press the start button on the computer base or tower – look for a light. This means that the computer is powering up (pressing again will turn the computer *off*)

- Press the button on the screen/monitor and look for a green light. This means that the monitor is on (pressing again will turn the monitor *off*)

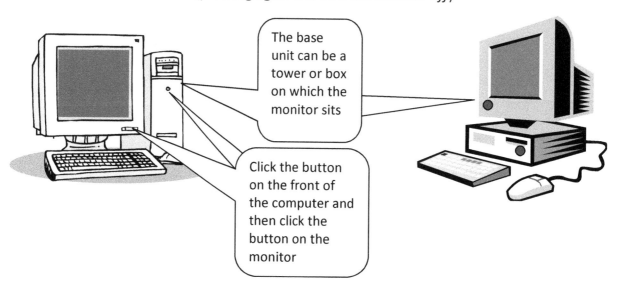

The base unit can be a tower or box on which the monitor sits

Click the button on the front of the computer and then click the button on the monitor

- Wait for Microsoft® Windows to load and then enter your username and password.

Log off and shut down a computer

- Make sure that all windows and programs are closed and that you have logged off any sites that you have visited

- Click the **Start** button on the task bar and then click **Log Off**

- A message may ask if you want to log off the system; click Yes
- Or, if you haven't used a username and password to enter Microsoft® Windows, select the **Start** button and then click **Shut Down**. Click Yes to exit the computer.

Activity 1.1 - Have a Go 👍

Getting Started

- Start the computer and make sure that the monitor is also active
- Enter a username and password if the login box appears, and click OK
- Microsoft Windows® will open.
- Click the Start button and then Shut Down.
- Click Yes to shut down the computer

Getting Started Checklist

Activity	Tick ✓ when complete
Computer is on	☐
Monitor is on	☐
Logged in with username and password	☐
Microsoft Windows is open and the desktop is displayed	☐
Computer is shut down	☐
Computer and monitor are turned off	☐

Password Security

What does it mean?

Passwords are used to increase the security of information. A password is entered to log on to a computer system in a college or at work and also to withdraw cash from a cash machine (called ATMs). The password used to access a bank account is called a PIN (Personal Identification Number).

A password should be changed regularly and kept secret. It is important that you use a strong password. This means using random letters, symbols and numbers that cannot be easily guessed.

An example of a strong password: **TnJKL18$*@**

A weak password is one that can be easily guessed or 'cracked' by a fraudster. Examples of weak passwords are:

- Mother's maiden name
- Your date of birth
- Your birthplace
- Your name
- The word 'password'
- Using the top line on the keyboard (e.g. QWERTY or 123456)

Never give your password to anyone else. A bank will never ask you to give them your password, so do not reply to requests via email for your personal details or password. This is likely to be a scam called *phishing* which is used in identity theft.

Activity 1.2 - Have a Go

Staying Secure

- On a piece of paper, write down an example of a strong password and a weak password

- Write down the name of the password used to access a cash machine

- TRUE or FALSE: You should share your password with other people

  o True ☐

  o False ☐

Document Security

What does it mean?

Some documents are confidential or contain sensitive information which should only be seen by specified users. Document passwords are added to make sure that unauthorised users can not access or make changes to a document. When a password is typed in it is displayed as **** or ••••••. This is to ensure the privacy and security of the password.

Help Sheet - Handy Tips

Password protect a document
- Select **Save As** from the **File** tab and then, from the Save As dialog box, select the **Tools** button.
- Select **General Options** from the menu. Enter a password to open the file or a password to modify the file.
- Confirm the password and click OK.
- Select **Save** to save the file with password protection

Open a password protected document
- Select **Open** from the **File** tab and then select the document to be opened.
- Click **Open**.
- Enter the password when prompted and click OK.

Activity 1.3 - Have a Go

Staying Protected

- Write a brief explanation stating why document protection is important

- When you type in a password it is displayed as: ••••••

- Explain why passwords are displayed like this.

Health & Safety

What does it mean?

Health and safety is important when using a computer so that you don't put too much strain on your body by doing the following:

- X   spending too much time at the computer without breaks – can cause back, neck and shoulder strain and headaches

- X   straining your eyes or squinting against glare from bad lighting – can cause eye strain and headaches

- X   sitting for too long or using a chair that isn't adjustable – can cause neck, back and shoulder pain

- X   sitting at a desk which is the wrong height for you or doesn't have enough space to work on – can cause back, neck and shoulder pain

- X   typing for too long or typing with wrists in the wrong position – can cause Repetitive Strain Injury (RSI) in the wrists

- X   using the mouse for too long – can cause Carpal Tunnel Syndrome, another type of RSI

Making sure that the equipment you use is adjusted to suit you and prevent strain is called **ergonomics**. Using a computer incorrectly and without breaks can cause pain and injury – this is referred to as **physical stress**.

To prevent physical stress, do the following:

- ✓   Take regular breaks

- ✓   Make sure that your chair is adjusted to the right height for you

- ✓   Make sure that you use wrist rests and that your keyboard is positioned correctly so that you are sitting comfortable whilst typing

- ✓   Make sure that there is enough room on your desk to hold a document holder so that you don't have to look down whilst typing

- ✓   Make sure that there is enough lighting

- ✓   Make sure that there is no window glare by using blinds

- ✓   Use an ergonomic mouse if possible

Hazards

It is important that your work area is free from hazards, such as trailing wires, open drawers, items balanced on the edge of desks, walkways obstructed by objects, items placed at a height you cannot reach, cups holding liquid placed by electrical equipment, sharp objects on the edge of desks.

Activity 1.4 - Have a Go 👍

Staying Safe

- Look around you at your work area – can you see any hazards?
- Write down 2 hazards that you can see
- Write down the name of the injury caused by repetitive use of a keyboard or mouse
- Write a short sentence describing **ergonomics** and how it affects you

Staying Safe Checklist

Hazards	Tick ✓ if you see hazard
Walkway obstructed	☐
Trailing wires	☐
Open drawers	☐
Items balanced on the edge of desks	☐
Items placed at a height you cannot reach	☐
Cups holding liquid placed by electrical equipment	☐
Sharp objects on the edge of desks.	☐

Interface Features

What does it mean?

An interface is something that allows you to interact with an ICT system, such as the desktop in Microsoft Windows® 7 or the screen on a mobile phone.

An ATM machine (Automatic Teller Machine or cash dispenser) also contains a user interface where the customer can press buttons on-screen or on a keypad to withdraw cash or view their bank balance. Interface features include the following:

- Icons
- Windows
- Menus
- Dialog boxes
- Buttons

An interface is something that you can touch, click, speak to or press to see or hear a result

Help Sheet - Handy Tips ✋

Icons:

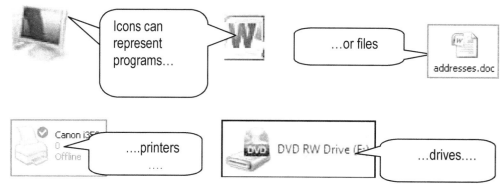

Icons can represent programs...

...or files

addresses.doc

Canon i35
0
Offline

....printers
....

DVD RW Drive (E:)

...drives....

Lorna's Docs

...or folders....

Tip:

An icon represents a program, file, printer, drive or folder. To open a file, folder or program, double click the icon or right click and select **Open**.

Window

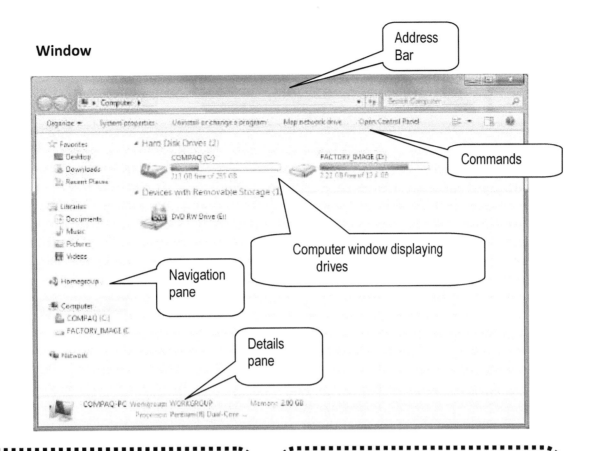

Address Bar

Commands

Computer window displaying drives

Navigation pane

Details pane

Tip:

A window can be resized if needed. To resize, move the mouse pointer over the edge of the window and, when the mouse pointer turns into a double headed black arrow, drag to the required size.

Tip:

A window can be moved to another location on the screen. Point at the top of the window and drag to the desired location.

Windows Buttons

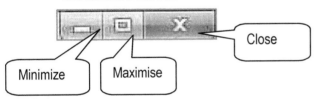

Close

Minimize

Maximise

Tip: When a window is maximised, the Maximise button turns into the *Restore* button. When clicked, the window is restored to its original size:

Scrollbars

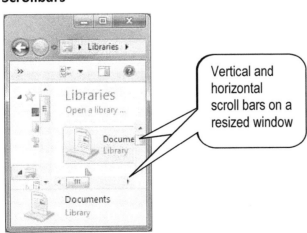

Vertical and horizontal scroll bars on a resized window

Tip:
The scroll bars will only appear when the window is resized and items within the window are obscured

9

Menus

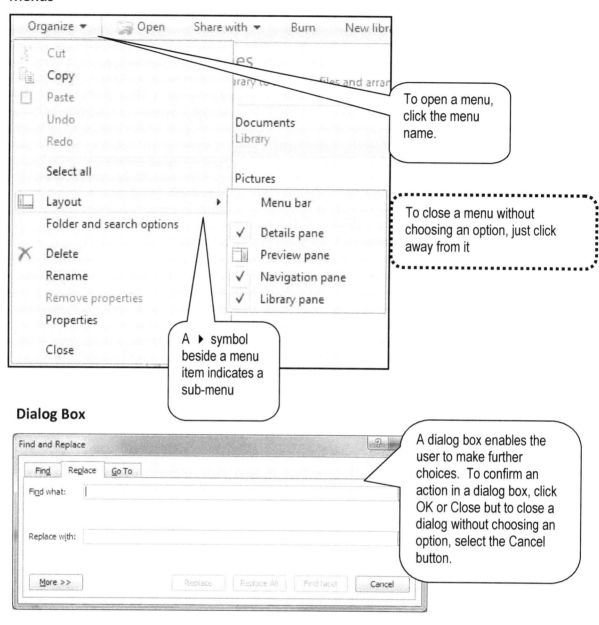

To open a menu, click the menu name.

To close a menu without choosing an option, just click away from it

A ▸ symbol beside a menu item indicates a sub-menu

Dialog Box

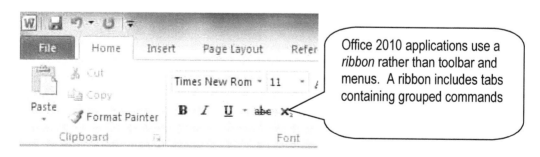

A dialog box enables the user to make further choices. To confirm an action in a dialog box, click OK or Close but to close a dialog without choosing an option, select the Cancel button.

Ribbon

Office 2010 applications use a *ribbon* rather than toolbar and menus. A ribbon includes tabs containing grouped commands

Common to all Office 2010 applications:
The **File** tab contains commonly used options, such as Open and Save:

The Quick Access Toolbar contains the Save and Undo/Redo buttons. Other buttons can be added as required:

Tabs replace menus: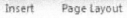

Each tab contains a ribbon with grouped commands:

Some of the groups contain a Dialog Box Launcher icon which, when clicked, will open a dialog box:

Zoom Bar

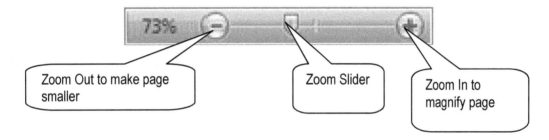

Zoom Out to make page smaller

Zoom Slider

Zoom In to magnify page

Activity 1.5 - Have a Go 👍

Identify features

What is the picture below:

1) A Window ☐   **2) An Icon** ☐   **3) A button** ☐   **4) A menu** ☐

Hardware

What does it mean?

Hardware is the term used for physical computer components which the user can touch. These include the actual computer and computer screen and the keyboard, mouse and printer (the latter three components are referred to as *peripherals*).

These are *hardware* components

Other items of hardware include:

- Scanner
- Digital camera
- Speakers

Activity 1.6 - Have a Go

Identify Hardware

- Look at your work area and count the amount of hardware items.

- On a piece of paper, write down the amount and the names of each piece of hardware you can see.

Software

What does it mean?

Software applications are computer programs designed to perform a particular task. For example:

Application Software

Word Processing

Word processed documents include the following:

- Letters
- Posters
- Newsletters
- Memorandums
- Timetables

An example of word processing software is Microsoft ® Office Word 2010.

Spreadsheets

A spreadsheet may be used for the following:

- Budgets
- Accounts
- Sales
- Invoices
- Timescales
- Charts

ITEM	AMOUNT	PRICE	TOTAL
Peas	2	.45	.90
Beans	1	.59	.59
Sugar	1	.89	.89
Tea	1	1.79	1.79
Bread	3	1.20	3.60
			7.77

An example of spreadsheet software is Microsoft® Office Excel 2010.

Presentations

A presentation when it is running is called a slide show. A slide show has the following uses:

- Display products and services in a continuously looping slide show in a reception area
- Present an idea to your boss
- Present a talk to a large audience
- Show hierarchical structures

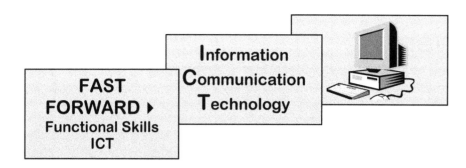

An example of presentation software is Microsoft ® Office PowerPoint 2010

Database

A database is an electronic filing system which enables the user to store data (such as friends' names and addresses) in a logical order. Examples of how a database may be used include:

- Storing and managing records
- Searching for specific records within a table
- Creating professional reports
- Using forms for data entry

An example of database software is Microsoft ® Office Access 2010

Web Browsing Software

Internet

The Internet is a network of interconnected computers which communicate globally with each other via an IP (Internet Protocol) Address. Using the Internet enables a user to access the World Wide Web (www). The World Wide Web is a collection of websites which are available on the Internet. Browsers include:

- Internet Explorer
- Netscape Navigator
- Mozilla Firefox
- Google Chrome

Communications Software

Email

Email software (Electronic Mail) provides a mailbox with an Inbox to receive mail. Users can receive, send, reply and forward mail with or without file attachments. Lists of friends' email addresses can be stored in a Contacts list.

Users may use web mail which allows them access to their mail on any computer with Internet access wherever they are in the world. Email software includes:

- Microsoft® Outlook Express
- Microsoft® Outlook 2003/2007/2010

Multi-media Software

Music

Music software allows a user to listen to music, purchase tracks and download them and make play lists of favourite mixes/tracks.

Video

Media software (media players) enable a user to download and view video. Most modern mobile phones and digital cameras have video capability, enabling video clips to be taken, with varying picture and sound quality, and then downloaded onto a computer.

Multi-media software includes:
- Apple QuickTime Player
- Apple iTunes
- Microsoft® Windows Media Player

Picture Editing Software

Photo Editing

Picture and photo editing software enables a user to edit, format and save pictures and photographs. Picture editing software includes:

- Adobe Photoshop
- Corel Paint Shop Pro
- Macromedia FireWorks
- CorelDraw Graphics

Checklist:
✓ Application software includes word processing, spreadsheets, databases, presentations
✓ Communications software includes e-mail
✓ Software that enables a user to browse the Internet is called a web browser
✓ Graphics software is used to edit and format pictures and photographs
✓ Multi-media software enables a user to download video and audio files

---

Activity 1.7 - Have a Go 👍

Software

- Write down the names of the software applications that are stored on your computer

- TRUE or FALSE: software refers to physical components that you can touch?

TRUE ☐   FALSE ☐

Working with Files

What does it mean?

A file is a document which has been created and saved on a computer, such as one of the following:

- A letter created using a word processing application
- A list of names and addresses stored in a database
- A monthly budget created using a spreadsheet
- A slide show created using presentation software

Saved files are represented by icons:

	A spreadsheet created and saved using Microsoft® Office Excel 2010		A document created and saved using Microsoft® Office Word 2010
	A presentation created and saved using Microsoft® Office PowerPoint 2010		A database created and saved using Microsoft® Office Access 2010

A file should be saved with an appropriate name to make it easier to locate and access. An example of a bad file name is **Doc 1.** This filename is not sufficiently descriptive and could relate to any file. A good filename is one that is descriptive, enabling the user to recognise and identify the file. A file is saved with a file extension to indicate the type of application in which it is saved:

- DOCX is the file extension for Microsoft® Office Word files
- XLSX is the file extension for Microsoft® Office Excel files
- ACCDB is the file extension for Microsoft® Office Access files
- PPTX is the file extension for Microsoft® Office PowerPoint files

Help Sheet - Handy Tips ✋

Create a new file
- Select the **File** tab and then **New**
- Select **Blank ......** (document, workbook etc depending on the type of application you are using). Select **Create**

Open a file
- Select the **File** tab and then select **Open**
- From the **Address Bar** drop down list select the correct location in which the file is stored
- Select the file and click **Open**

! To open a file from the Documents window, double click the file icon.

Save and close a file

Save
- Select the **File** tab and then select **Save** (or click the **Save** button on the Quick Access Toolbar)

Save As
- Select the **File** tab and then select **Save As**
- Ensure that the correct drive/folder is selected in the Address Bar
- Enter a name in the **File name** box and click **Save**

Close
- Select the **File** tab and then select **Close**

Activity 1.8 - Have a Go 👍

Create your first document

- Open Microsoft Word
- Create a new document
- Save the file as MyFirstFile
- Close the file

Input and Output Devices

What does it mean?

Input

Input devices are devices that enable a user to enter, store and select data or choose options from a menu which include:

- Mouse
- Keyboard
- Microphone
- Scanner

Output

Output devices display the results of input in the form of on-screen display or printed output. For example, a printed document is output. Examples of output devices include:

- Printer
- Monitor
- Speakers

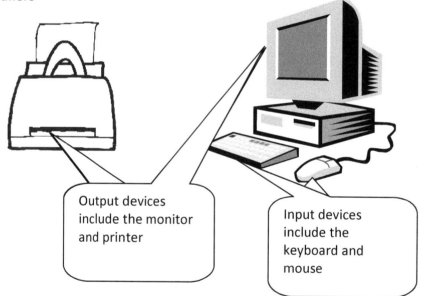

Output devices include the monitor and printer

Input devices include the keyboard and mouse

Help Sheet - Handy Tips ✋

Using the Keyboard

Enter text

- The flashing black line at the top of a document is called the *cursor*. This is where the text will appear as you type. To create a capital letter (UPPER CASE), hold down the **Shift** key whilst pressing the key on the keyboard. For example, Keyboard, is typed with the initial letter in capitals or upper case. Click the cursor into position and start typing. Existing text will move along the line to accommodate the new text being entered.
- Press the spacebar to create a space between words as you type.
- To use the symbols above the number keys, hold down the **Shift** key and press the key that you want, e.g. !"£$%^&*()_+
- Press the **ENTER** key to create a new paragraph

Delete text

One character at a time

- Position the cursor in front of text and press the Delete key or position cursor at the end of text and use the Backspace key (the Delete key deletes text to the right of the current cursor position and Backspace deletes text to the left of the cursor position). Pressing the Delete or Backspace key once will delete a single character or space. Repeat to delete multiple characters/spaces.

Whole word

- Position the cursor in front of the word. Hold down the **CTRL** key on the keyboard and then press the Delete key. Position the cursor at the end of the word, hold down the **CTRL** key and press the Backspace key.

Using the mouse

Undo and Redo

- The Quick Access Toolbar displays the Undo and Redo buttons.
- Click the Undo button to undo an action. Click the Redo button to re-do an action

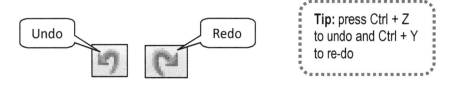

Undo   Redo

Tip: press Ctrl + Z to undo and Ctrl + Y to re-do

Print

- Select the **File** tab and then select **Print**.
- Select **Quick Print** to print the document without making changes
- Select **Print** to make changes before printing and then click the **Print** button.

Activity 1.9 - Have a Go 👍

Enter text and print a document

- Open the document that you saved called **MyFirstFile**
- Enter your name at the top of the document
- Save the document
- Print the document
- Close the document

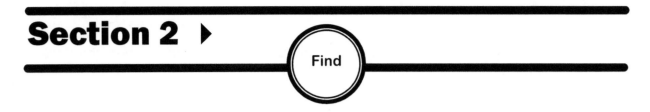

Section 2 ▶

Find

Finding and Selecting Information

Sources of ICT Information

What does it mean?

Although the Internet is an easy to access and varied source of information, there are many other non-ICT based information sources available:

Non-ICT Information Sources
- Newspapers, magazines, books
- Images, diagrams, maps
- Conversations, text messages

ICT Information sources:
- CDs and DVDs (encyclopaedias, documentaries, language courses)
- Websites such as wikis, podcasts, weblogs (blogs), web-based reference sites (webopaedias)

Activity 2.1 - Have a Go

Find information

- Look in your local library for sources of information on using Office 2010

- Look on the magazine shelves of your local shop or supermarket and count the amount of magazines that provide information about technology (computers, digital cameras etc)

Using the Find tool

What does it mean?

The **Find** tool is common to each of the Microsoft® Office applications and is used to find part or whole words or phrases within a document. This is a handy tool which helps to save time by searching through long documents for a search word. The **Find** tool can also be used to find text on a web page.

Microsoft Office

- Open a Microsoft® Office application, e.g. Microsoft® Word, Microsoft® Excel, Microsoft® PowerPoint or Microsoft® Access
- Select the **Home** tab and then, from the **Editing** group, select the **Find** command
- Enter the search criteria into the **Find What** box and click **Find Next**. Continue clicking **Find Next** until each occurrence of the search word has been located

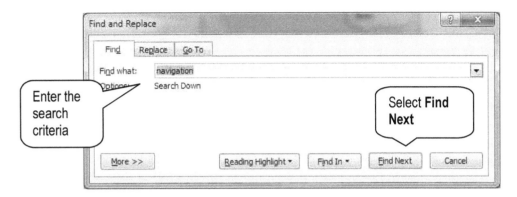

Microsoft Internet Explorer

- Select the **Edit** menu and then select **Find on this page** (if the menu bar is missing, hold down the **Alt** key). Alternatively, hold down **CTRL** and press **F**

- Enter the search criteria within the **Find** box and click **Next**. Continue clicking **Next** until each occurrence of the search word has been found

- The search words will be highlighted on the web page and the amount of matches displayed on the Find bar:

Using Windows Search tools

Did You Know?

File searching can be performed using partial file names

What does it mean?

The Search facility in Microsoft Windows allows the user to search for files and folders using partial file names, file types, file sizes, date saved, or file location.

This feature is very handy when you can't find a file and only know that it starts with a 'p', is a Microsoft Word document and was saved on a specific date.

Help Sheet - Handy Tips ✋

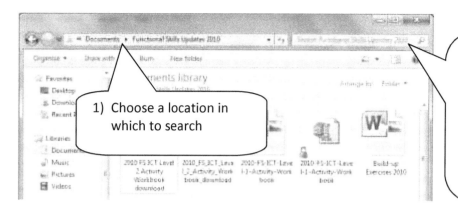

1) Choose a location in which to search

2) Enter the file name here and, as you type, a list of files containing the typed characters is listed below (e.g. if you type **data**, all files containing these characters will be listed

3) As you type, the **Add a search filter** menu opens. Click a search filter to search by author, date modified, file type or file size.

Activity 2.2 - Have a Go 👍

Search for files

- Using the Search tool, find the document that you saved earlier called **MyFirstFile.doc**
- Open the file
- Close the file.

Using the Internet

What does it mean?

The Internet is a vast collection of computers that are connected over a global network.

The World Wide Web is a collection of web sites which can be accessed via the Internet. A web site contains one or more web pages which are linked together. The start page in a website is called a Home Page. To gain access to the Internet, a user must have the following:

- Computer
- Telephone line
- Modem or router
- Web browser software (e.g. Microsoft® Internet Explorer, Mozilla Firefox etc)

An ISP (Internet Service Provider) provides Internet connection for a fee. There are many ISPs available, such as BT, AOL, Talk Talk and many others, all providing connectivity services at differing prices and Internet speeds. There are different types of Internet connection:

- Broadband – allows use of the telephone whilst online; monthly fee

- Dial-up – telephone line unavailable whilst online; pay for what you use

- WIFI – wireless connection enabling connection to the Internet whilst mobile

- Pay-As-You-Go – pre-paid Internet connection using an adapter, called a Dongle, which is inserted into the USB port of a computer

To access the Internet, you need a *web browser*, such as Internet Explorer.

Web Addresses

A web address is the address of a website which, when entered into the Address Bar in a web browser, will find and open the first page within the website (called the Home Page). A web address is also called a URL (Uniform Resource Locator).

An example of a web address is:

All web addresses or URLs start with Http:// (stands for HyperText Transfer Protocol and this is entered automatically)

http://www.google.co.uk

World Wide Web

The domain name and geographical location

Search Engines

A search engine is an Internet search tool which is designed to search within its vast database for keywords or phrases (called search criteria) entered by a user into a search engine box. A list of web page links that match the keywords, in order of relevance, will be displayed. When clicked, a webpage link will open a webpage which contains one or more of the keywords. One example of a search engine is **www.google.co.uk.**

Help Sheet - Handy Tips ✋

Access the Internet
- Select the **Start** button and **All Programs** (unless displayed in the Start menu) and then select **Microsoft® Internet Explorer** or double click the icon on the desktop.

Internet
Explorer

Enter a URL
- Click the cursor into the Address Bar at the top of the web page and enter the URL:

http://www.google.co.uk/

- For example, to access the Google™ UK search engine, enter:

All web addresses or URLs start with Http:// (stands for HyperText Transfer Protocol and this is entered automatically)

http://www.google.co.uk

World Wide Web

The domain name and geographical location

- Press Enter or click the green arrow to go to the URL or click the X to stop the page from downloading.

Use a Search Engine
- Click the cursor into the search box and enter the search criteria, i.e. keyword or phrase.
- Press the Enter key or click the **Search** button (if using Google™ UK, click **Google Search)**.
- A list of web pages will be displayed in order of relevance. Click a link to see the web page.

Google ™
UK

Advanced Search
Language Tools

Google Search | I'm Feeling Lucky

Search: ○ the web ⊙ pages from the UK

Save an image on a web page
- Right click an image, diagram or map on a web page. Select **Save Picture As**. Select the correct location in which to save the image and click **Save.**

© Qualiteach Education, 2012

Activity 2.3 - Have a Go 👍

Use a Web browser

- Using a web browser, enter **www.google.co.uk** into the Address Bar and press Enter
- Enter the keywords **Functional Skills** into the Google search engine
- Open a web page which gives information about Functional Skills
- Close the web page
- Close the web browser

Section 3 ▶

Data

Develop Information

Enter & Edit Data

What does it mean?

For entering data see Section 1 – page 17. *For more help on editing data, e.g. deleting text, see Section 1 page 17*

Cut, Copy and Paste

- Before text can be copied or moved it must first be selected. Position the cursor within a word and double click the left mouse button to select the whole word. Alternatively, position cursor in front of text and then, holding down the left mouse button, drag the mouse over the text to highlight (select) it.
- **To copy text**: select the **Copy** button From the **Home** tab and the **Clipboard** group
- **To cut text**: select the **Cut** button From the **Home** tab and the **Clipboard** group
- Position the cursor in the new location on the page and then click the **Paste** button (**Home** tab and **Clipboard** group)

Paste — *Cut* — *Copy*

Check Spelling

- **Microsoft® Word, Excel and PowerPoint**: From the **Review** tab and the **Proofing** group, select the **Spelling & Grammar** command (Word) or the **Spelling** command (Excel, PowerPoint).
- **Microsoft® Access**: From the **Home** tab and the **Proofing** group, select the **Spelling** command ✎ Spelling
- The Spelling tool will display spelling errors and provide suggested replacements. Select a suggestion or click **Ignore** if you know that the word is correct (click **Ignore All** to ignore all instances of the word or **Change All** to change each instance of the word to the suggested spelling). A dialog box will appear at completion of the spelling check. Click OK to confirm.

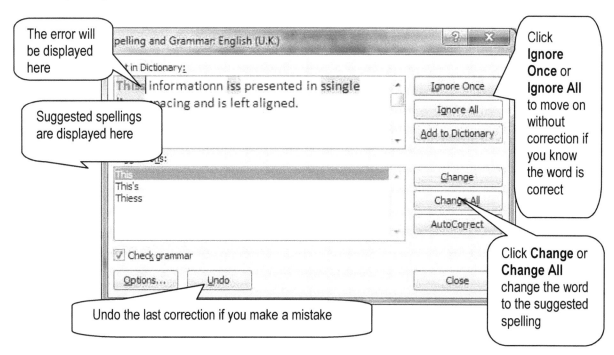

The error will be displayed here

Suggested spellings are displayed here

Click **Ignore Once** or **Ignore All** to move on without correction if you know the word is correct

Click **Change** or **Change All** change the word to the suggested spelling

Undo the last correction if you make a mistake

Format Data

What does it mean?

Formatting means making text look more attractive or making it stand out. Formatting can include changing the font, size, colour and style:

ALGERIAN FONT IN SIZE 24 WITH BOLD, ITALICS AND UNDERLINE

Formatting also refers to changing the alignment, such as left, right and centre:

> **This text is centred**
> **This text is left aligned**
> **This text is right aligned**

Lists can be formatted with numbers and bullets:

- This is a bullet
1. This is numbered

Help Sheet - Handy Tips

Formatting Techniques

Fonts, sizes, styles and colour

- Select the text to be formatted and then select a font type, font size, font style (bold, italics, underline) or font colour from the **Font** group (**Home** tab).

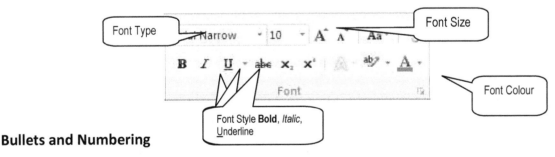

Font Type — Font Size — Font Colour — Font Style **Bold**, *Italic*, Underline

Bullets and Numbering

- Highlight the list and then select the **Bullets** or **Numbering** button from the **Home** tab and the **Paragraph** group.

Line Spacing

- Select the text or position the cursor within a paragraph and then select the **Line Spacing** button from the **Home** tab and the **Paragraph** group. Select an option from the drop down menu.

Alignment

- Select the text and then select one of the **Alignment** buttons from the **Home** tab and the **Paragraph** group (the alignment options are: left, centre, right, justify in Microsoft® Word and PowerPoint and Left, Centre and Right in Microsoft® Excel and Access).

Left, Centre, Right, Justify

Layout Techniques

Margins

- **Microsoft® Word, Excel:** select the **Margins** button from the **Page Layout** tab and the **Page Setup** group. Choose a margin setting or select **Custom Margins** to choose your own margin sizes.
- The **Page Setup** dialog box will appear. Select the top, bottom, left and right margins and click **OK**

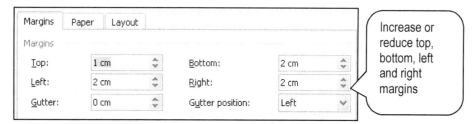

Increase or reduce top, bottom, left and right margins

- **Microsoft® Access:** select the **File** tab, **Print** and then **Print Preview.** Select the **Margins** button. Choose a margin setting from the drop down list. To choose different margin settings, click the **Page Layout** dialog box launcher icon. From the **Print Options** tab, select margins as required and click OK.

Orientation

- **Microsoft® Word, Excel:** from the **Page Layout** tab, select **Orientation**. Choose Portrait or Landscape
- **Microsoft® PowerPoint:** From the **Design** tab, select the **Slide Orientation** button and choose an orientation from the drop down list.
- **Microsoft® Access:** select the **File** tab, **Print** and then **Print Preview.** Select either **Portrait** or **Landscape** buttons from the **Page Layout** group

Choose an orientation

Print Preview

- To check your document for layout and correct page structure, select the **File** tab and then select the **Print** button. Your document will be previewed in the right hand pane.
- Print the document by clicking the **Print** button or exit Print Preview by selecting the **File** tab.

Page Border

- For a page border, select the **Page Border** button from the **Page Layout** tab and **Page Background** group. Select a style, colour and width or click the **Art** list arrow and choose a style.

Activity 3.1 - Have a Go 👍

Enter, Edit and Format Text

- Open a new document and enter your name at the top
- Enter the following text (including the deliberate spelling mistakes) beneath your name:

  The kat satt onn the matt. The rane in Spain falls mainly on the plain.

- Use the Spelling tool to correct the errors.
- Delete the first sentence.
- Format the text in a different font, size and colour of your choice.
- Centre the text.
- Save the document as **Edit.doc** and close.

Insert Pictures

What does it mean?

Graphics are images or pictures which can be inserted from the Clipart gallery, from a Clipart image DVD or from a stored location on your computer (such as digital photographs).

Help Sheet - Handy Tips ✋

Insert Clip Art
- Position the cursor where the image is to be inserted. Select the **Insert** tab.
- Select the **Clip Art** button and the Clip Art task pane will open.
- Type an image name/description into the **Search for** box (e.g. computer) and press the **Go** button. The Clip Art gallery will display images matching the search words that you entered. Select an image to insert it into the document or slide.

Insert an image from file
- Position the cursor in the document or slide where the image is to be inserted. Select the **Insert** tab.
- Select the **Picture** button and the **Insert Picture** dialog box will appear.
- Find and select the required image file and then click **Insert.**

Resize an image

- Click the image and resizing handles will appear around the image.
- Move the mouse pointer over a corner resizing handle (always drag from a corner handle to maintain image proportions) and drag inwards and downwards to reduce the size or outwards and upwards to increase the size.
- Images can also be resized accurately by selecting **Shape Height** or **Shape Width** measurements from the **Picture Tools/Format** tab and the **Size** group. Choose whether to change the height or width measurement.

Align an image

- Select the image. From the **Home** tab and the **Paragraph** group, select an Alignment button.

Move an Image

- Position mouse pointer over image, hold down mouse button (black cross icon appears) and drag to desired location on the page.

Activity 3.2 - Have a Go 👍

Insert an image

- Create a new document

- Insert an image from Clipart

- Resize it as required

- Centre the image

- Save the document as **Mypicture**

- Close the document

Drawing Tools

What does it mean?

Drawing tools are used to create shapes, such as circles, ovals, squares, text boxes, arrows etc.

See the examples below:

Rectangle

square

Oval

Circle

Examples

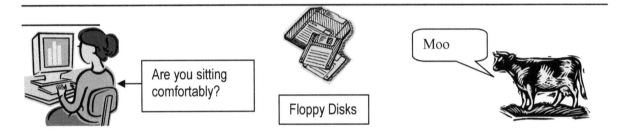

Are you sitting comfortably?

Floppy Disks

Moo

Help Sheet - Handy Tips

Create Shapes

- Select the **Insert** tab and then, from the **Illustrations** group, select the **Shapes** command.
- Choose a shape from the drop-down menu.
- Position the mouse pointer on the page where the shape is to be inserted.
- The mouse pointer displays as a black crosshair icon
- Either click the mouse to insert the shape or drag the shape to the required size

Shapes

Tip: Hold down the **Shift** key when creating a rectangle or oval shape to create a perfect square or circle

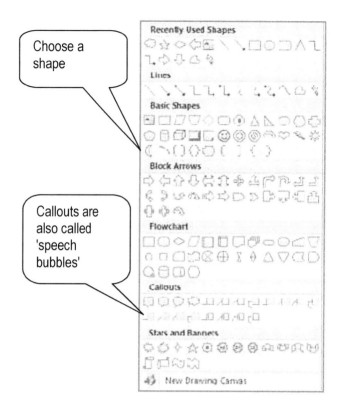

Insert Text

- Right click the shape and select **Add Text**. The cursor will be positioned within the shape.
- Enter the text.

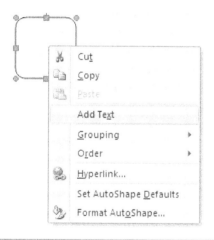

Activity 3.3 - Have a Go 👍

Create shapes

- Create a new document

- Create a shape

- Resize it as required

- Add your name to the shape

- Save the document as **Myshape**

- Close the document

Work with Numbers

Did You Know?

The section between a row and a column is called a cell

What does it mean?

A spreadsheet is used for performing calculations and is displayed as a grid containing rows and columns. The rows are horizontal and the columns are vertical.

A row is numbered and a column is lettered (e.g. column A and row 1). There are many rows and columns in a spreadsheet. Both rows and columns can be deleted if required or extra rows/columns inserted. The intersection between a row and a column is called a cell. The name of the cell is made up of the column letter and the row number (e.g. cell A1) and is referred to as a cell reference. Calculations in a spreadsheet are created using cell references rather than the numerical data. For example:

=A1+B1   instead of   =2+10

This ensures that, when the numbers change, the formula re-calculates.

Every formula starts with the equals sign = and uses arithmetic operators for addition, subtraction, division and multiplication:

+	Addition
-	Subtraction
/	Division
*	Multiplication

	A	B	C	D
1	Item	Amount	Cost	Total
2	Mouse	2	9.99	=B2*C2
3	Keyboard	1	14.99	=B3*C3
4	Memory stick	3	12.99	=B4*C4

The total cost of purchases uses the multiplication operator to multiply the cost by the amount (note how cell references are used

Multiple cells are referred to as a cell range. The cell range, when used in a formula uses the first and last cell in the range separated by a colon : (e.g. A1:C10). Cell ranges are used in formulas and functions in the following way:

=SUM(B3:B7)   this formula uses the SUM function to find the total of the cell range B3 to B7

	A	B
1	Ryan's 18th Birthday Party	
2		
3	Venue	£150.00
4	Catering	£350.00
5	Entertainment	£250.00
6	Postal costs	£10.00
7		
8	Total Costs	£760.00

Help Sheet - Handy Tips ✋

Enter data
- Click into a cell to select it. The selected cell will display a black border. Type in the text or numbers and then press Enter or use the keyboard arrow keys to move to the next cell.

Cell Data Types
- Select the cells or cell range to be formatted. Select one of the commands shown (Home tab and the Number group):

Choose Currency, Percentage, Comma, Increase or decrease decimals

Alternatively, to see the **Format Cells** dialog box, select the dialog box launcher icon

Cell Formatting
- Select the cells and then choose a formatting option from the Font group (fonts, sizes, styles, colour, cell fill colour, cell borders).

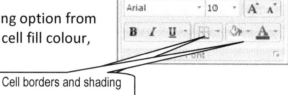

Cell borders and shading

Create a Formula
- Enter the **Equals** sign (=) followed by the first cell reference. Enter the arithmetic operator, such as +, -, /, * followed by the second cell reference (e.g. =A1*B1).

Use the AutoSum Function
- Click into the cell in which the result will be displayed. Select the AutoSum button (Home tab and Editing group). The SUM formula (e.g. =SUM(A1:C10) will display on the spreadsheet; click the AutoSum button again to complete the function.
- You can also enter a SUM function manually: type the equals sign (=), followed by the function name SUM. Type an open round bracket and then type the cell range separated by a colon (:). Close the bracket, e.g. =SUM(A1:C10).

Page Layout
- Commands such as Margins, Orientation (Portrait/Landscape) can be selected from the **Page Layout** tab and the **Page Setup** group. For other page layout options, such as headers and footers and to display gridlines and/or row and column headings, click the dialog box launcher icon to open the **Page Setup** dialog box.

Activity 3.4 - Have a Go 👍

Create a spreadsheet

Exercise 1

- Create a new spreadsheet and enter your name in cell A1

- In cell B3 enter the text **Tickets Sold**

- In cell A4 enter the text **Summer 2009**

- In cell A5 enter the text **Summer 2010**

- In cell B4 enter the number 1500

- In cell B5 enter the number 1800

- In cell A6 enter the text **Total**

- In cell B6 enter a formula to find the total tickets sold (tip: use + or SUM)

- Save the spreadsheet as **Sales** and close

Example

	A	B
1	Candidate Name	
2		
3		Tickets Sold
4	Summer 2009	1500
5	Summer 2010	1800
6	Total	3300

Exercise 2

- Create a new spreadsheet and enter your name in cell A1

- In cell A2 enter the text: **Winter 2012 Ticket Price**

- In cell B2 enter the ticket price **£5.55**

- Save the spreadsheet as **Ticket** and close

Section 4 ▶

View

Combine and present information

Combine Information

What does it mean?

Combined information means bringing together bits of data from different sources, such as text, numbers and images. For example, creating a poster or creating a presentation.

Poster containing formatted text, image and numbers (price)

Before combining information think about how it will be viewed. Will it be displayed on-screen as a PowerPoint slide show or as a web page, or will it be printed as a paper copy?

If you are creating a poster that is to be printed and displayed, you will need to think about the print quality and the cost of paper and printer ink (to print in colour, the printer needs a colour cartridge installed which is more expensive than a black toner cartridge).

If you are creating an on-screen slide show, then you don't need to worry about paper or printer ink, but you do need to think about how the colours and images display on a monitor or projector.

Help Sheet - Handy Tips ✋

Switch between open windows
- Open files will display as tabs on the task bar. Click a tab to open the file. Alternatively, select the View tab and then click **Switch Windows**. Choose the file to open.
- Tip: A shortcut key combination for switching between windows is **Alt** and **Tab**.

Insert graphs/spreadsheet data using copy and paste
- Open Excel and the file containing the graph/data. Select the graph or spreadsheet data to be copied and click the **Copy** button from the **Clipboard** group.
- Switch to the open document and select **Paste**.

See **Section 3 Insert Pictures** for help on inserting Clipart pictures or images from file.

Activity 4.1 - Have a Go 👍

Create a poster

- Create a new document and save it as **poster**
- Enter the heading **CHARITY DISCO**
- Beneath the heading enter the following text: **at Bramton Village Hall, Saturday 30th October**
- Insert a suitable Clipart image such as a dancer, glitterball etc. Centre the image and resize it if necessary
- Beneath the image enter the text: **Call Neela on 01234 567890 for tickets**
- Beneath the telephone number enter the following text: **Ticket Price:**
- Open the spreadsheet you saved earlier as **Ticket**
- Copy the ticket price from the spreadsheet and paste into the poster after the text **Ticket Price:**
- Make the poster look attractive by formatting the text with different fonts, sizes and colour. Use shapes, such as the star shape shown below to enhance the poster.
- Save the poster and close

Example

Accuracy and Meaning

What does it mean?

It is important to check your work carefully before printing or displaying it to others. This can be by using the Spelling tool to check for spelling errors, reading through your work to check each word (this is called *proofreading*) and checking that layout is suitable by previewing the document.

In addition to accuracy, it is also important to make sure that the meaning you are trying to convey is clear. Will viewers of your combined document or presentation understand what it is about? For example, a poster for a party will use different wording as well as a different layout and style to a formal business letter.

Presentations

What does it mean?

A presentation is a set of slides which are presented in a specific order to an audience or as a continuously looping presentation in a reception area. A presentation which is presented to an audience is called a slide show.

Help Sheet - Handy Tips ✋

See **Section 3 Insert Pictures** for help on inserting Clipart pictures or images from file.

Create a Master Slide

- Select the Slide Master button from the View tab and the Presentation Views group

- Format the slide areas as desired (select formatting tools from the Home tab

Apply Background Colour

- Ensure that Master Slide view is selected. Select the **Background Styles** button. Select **Format Background**. Select the **Color** button and choose a colour. Click **Apply to All**. Click **Close**.

Insert New Slide

- Ensure that Normal view is selected and then select the **New Slide** button from the **Home** tab. Select a slide layout.

Change Slide Layout

- In Normal view, select the **Layout** button from the **Home** tab. Select a slide layout.

Print

- From the **File** tab select **Print**.

- To print each slide, ensure that the **Print All Slides** and **Full Page Slides** are both selected in the **Settings** section. Click **Print**.

Print handouts

- Select the **File** tab and then **Print**. From the Print window select the **Settings** arrow.

- From the **Handouts** pane, select the amount of slides. Click Print.

Activity 4.2 - Have a Go 👍

Create a slide

- Open PowerPoint and insert a new slide.

- Type your name as the title.

- Insert a clip art image of your choice below your name.

- Save the presentation as **MyPres** and close.

Section 5 ▶

Mail

Communicate Information

Open and Read an Email

What does it mean?

E-mail stands for Electronic Mail. An email is a means of communication via electronic mail which can be sent and received via a computer with an Internet connection, a phone line and a modem.

An Internet Service Provider (ISP) provides connectivity for a fee. There are many ISPs available from which to choose, each with varying costs and services.

A user can send a new message to one or more recipients (a recipient is someone who receives), reply to a message and forward messages.

Email addresses are entered into the **To:** field and separated by a semicolon (;). An example of an email address is **contact@qualiteach.co.uk**. The first part of an email address is the *username* followed by the @ (at) symbol. The next part of the address is called the *domain name*, which sometimes includes the geographical location (UK)

Help Sheet - Handy Tips

Read an E-mail
- The Inbox displays received messages. If the message is displayed in **Bold** it is unread. To open a message, double click it.

Reply to an email
- Received messages are displayed in the Inbox. Select the message to which you want to reply and then select the **Reply** button (the **Reply All** button will send a reply to all of the recipients of the original email). The original sender's email address will be displayed in the **To** field. Enter your text at the top of the message, above the original message details (To, From, Date etc). Click the **Send** button.

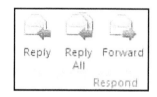

Forward an email
- Select the message that you want to forward to another recipient. Click the **Forward** button. Enter the email address or addresses in the **To:** field, separating addresses with a semi colon. Add an address or addresses to the **CC** field if you want to send a copy to that address. Enter an address or addresses into the **BCC** field if you don't want the other recipients of the message to see it. Enter your text above the original message details (To, From, Date etc). Click the **Send** button.

Create and Send an E-mail

- To create a new email message, select the **New E-mail** button from the **Home** tab or select **New Items** and then **E-mail Message**. Enter the email address or addresses (separated by a semi colon) in the **To** field or, to send a copy of the message to another recipient, add the address or addresses to the **CC** field. Enter the address or addresses into the **BCC** field if you don't want the other recipients of the message to see their address (click the **Options** tab and then **BCC**). Enter a subject for the message in the **Subject** box. Enter text into the message area. Click the **Send** button.

Activity 5.1 - Have a Go 👍

Create and send an email

- Create a new email using your own email address and the subject Charity Disco

- Enter the following text:

Hi
I hope you can come to the disco.

- Open the **Poster** document that you created earlier and copy the address and date of the charity disco into the email message.

- Enter your name beneath the email message

- Send the message.

Use Contacts

What does it mean?

Email addresses can be stored as contacts. A list of contacts is called a distribution list. Attaching a list of contacts is quicker and easier than entering each email address separately.

Example: email addresses, each entered separately 3 times:

john@qualiteach.co.uk
jane@qualiteach.co.uk
hardeep@qualiteach.co.uk

To: john@qualiteach.co.uk; jane@qualiteach.co.uk;
hardeep@qualiteach.co.uk

Example: list of email addresses, entered once

Friends_List

john@qualiteach.co.uk
jane@qualiteach.co.uk
hardeep@qualiteach.co.uk

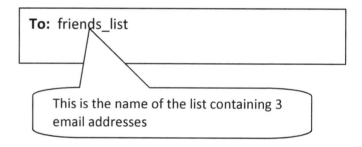

To: friends_list

This is the name of the list containing 3 email addresses

Help Sheet - Handy Tips

Create a Contact:
- Open an email message and right click the sender's email address. Select **Add to Outlook Contacts** and enter further details if needed, then click **Save and Close**. Alternatively, select the **Home** tab and then click **New Items** and then **Contact**. Enter details for the contact and click **Save and Close** (these instructions are assuming that you in Mail view; if you have chosen Contacts view, click the **New Contact** command.

Create a Contact/Distribution List:
- Select **Home ▸ New Items ▸ More Items ▸ Contact Group.** Type in a name for the list. Click the **Add Members** button. Choose **From Outlook Contacts.** Select the contacts that you want to include in the distribution list and then click the **Members** button. Repeat to add all contacts to the list. Click **OK.** Click **Save and Close** (these instructions are assuming that you in Mail view; if you have chosen Contacts view, click the **New Contact Group** command).

Edit or Delete a Contact:
- *Edit:* select Contacts from the navigation pane. A list of all your contacts will be displayed in the right hand pane. Double click a contact to make changes to the existing details and then click Save and Close.
- *Delete*: select Contacts from the navigation pane. A list of all your contacts will be displayed in the right hand pane. Right click a contact and then select Delete from the shortcut menu (alternatively select Delete from the Home tab/New group).

Add a Contacts List to an Email Message:
- Open a new message and select the **To** field. The **Select Names** dialog box opens. Select the contact group 🖧 and click the **To** button. Repeat to add other contacts or lists to the **CC** or **BCC** fields. Click OK. Enter a subject and the message text and then click **Send.**

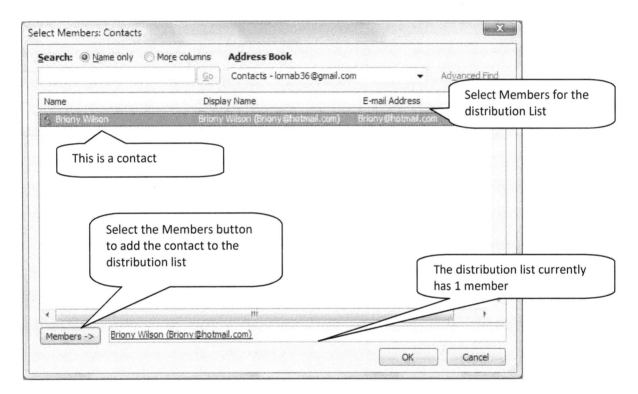

Stay safe and respect others

What does it mean?

Always use appropriate language when communicating on a social networking group or chat room/forum. Be careful not to use inflammatory or bad language or be insulting or disrespectful to others. Using bad language or language designed to make people angry is called **flaming** and can get a user banned from online forums. Be careful to respect the views of other people and be tolerant towards gender, age or cultural differences.

Always ask permission before communicating another person's views or opinions.

It has become increasingly important to take care of personal details since the advent of social networking sites (a social networking site is a site, such as Twitter or Facebook, where a user posts details about themselves and allows other people to communicate with them via instant messaging and email).

Users of social networking sites should be careful about what information they post about themselves and others.

Always ask permission before posting any information or photos of other people.

To prevent identity theft and fraudulent use of your personal details, it is good practice to limit the people who can view your personal details to specific friends and family members.

To avoid the possibility of a stranger using your details for fraudulent purposes, you should never provide the following information on a social networking site:

- Your address
- Your date of birth
- Photographs containing you or friends
- Telephone number
- Email address

Answers ▶

Mark

Answers to Activity questions

Activity 1.1

Computer is turned on and off using correct procedure

Activity 1.2

A strong password is a random mix of letters, numbers and symbols, e.g.:

TnJKL18$*@

A weak password is one that can be easily guessed or 'cracked' by a fraudster. Examples of weak passwords are:

- Mother's maiden name
- Your date of birth
- Your birthplace
- Your name
- The word 'password'
- Using the top line on the keyboard (e.g. QWERTY or 123456)

FALSE: you should NEVER share your password with other people

Activity 1.3

Some documents are confidential or contain sensitive information which should only be seen by specified users. Document passwords are added to make sure that unauthorised users can not access or make changes to a document.

When a password is typed in it is displayed as **** or ••••••. This is to ensure the privacy and security of the password.

Activity 1.4

A hazard could be: trailing wires, open drawers, items balanced on the edge of desks, walkways obstructed by objects, items placed at a height you cannot reach, cups holding liquid placed by electrical equipment, sharp objects on the edge of desks

Typing for too long or typing with wrists in the wrong position can cause Repetitive Strain Injury (RSI) in the wrists

Making sure that the equipment you use is adjusted to suit you and prevent strain is called *ergonomics*. Using a computer incorrectly and without breaks can cause pain and injury – this is referred to as **physical stress**.

Activity 1.5

2.   An icon

Activity 1.6

Hardware items could be: computer, mouse, keyboard, printer, scanner, speakers

Activity 1.7

Software programs could be: Web browser, email client, word processing, database, spreadsheet, presentations, desktop publishing etc

FALSE - hardware refers to physical components that you can touch; software refers to programs stored on the computer

Activity 1.8/9

File should be saved as MyFirstFile, the printout should display candidate name at the top of the document

Activities 2.1, 2.2 and 2.3

These do not require printing. For 2.1 the candidate should find sources of information about Office 2010 in their local library, e.g. books, journals, guides, DVDs, CDs, magazines, IT support staff. The candidate should count the amount of media available on technology in their local shop. For 2.2 the file **MyFirstFile** should be located and opened. For 2.3 the candidate should use Google or other search engine to find web pages which provide information on functional skills.

Activity 3.1

The text should read (after spelling check):

The cat sat on the mat. The rain in Spain falls mainly on the plain

The first sentence should be deleted and the remainder of text should read:

The rain in Spain falls mainly on the plain

Text should be formatted in a different font, size and colour of your choice. Centre the text:

The rain in Spain falls mainly on the plain

Activity 3.2

Image should be centred on the page. File saved as **Mypicture**

Activity 3.3

Shape should contain your name. File saved as **Myshape**

> My Name

Activity 3.4

Exercise 1: Spreadsheet should look like this:

	A	B
1	Candidate Name	
2		
3		Tickets Sold
4	Summer 2009	1500
5	Summer 2010	1800
6	Total	3300

Exercise 2: Spreadsheet should look like this:

	A	B
1	Candidate Name	
2	Winter 2012 Ticket Price	5.55
3		

Activity 4.1

Poster should look similar to this:

Activity 4.2

Slide should look something like this:

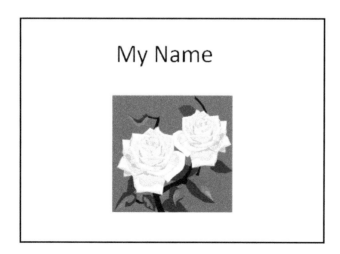

Activity 5.1

Subject: Charity Disco

Email should read:

Hi

I hope you can come to the disco at Bramton Village Hall, Saturday 30th October

My name

Lightning Source UK Ltd.
Milton Keynes UK
UKHW051832271119
354333UK00007B/375/P

9 780956 573131